C000203284

Unless otherwise noted, all scripture quotations are taken from the King James Version of the Bible.

*The Spirit of Leadership*
ISBN 1-931289-06-9

Bill Winston Ministries
P.O. Box 947
Oak Park, Illinois 60303-0947

# *The Spirit of*
# LEADERSHIP

BILL WINSTON

*The Spirit of Leadership*

# Table of Contents

**Introduction** ................................................................ **1**

**Chapter 1** **Leadership Begins with a Dream** ................. **5**

**Chapter 2** **What is a Leader** .......................................... **19**

**Chapter 3** **Barriers to Effective Leadership** ................ **33**

Boxed Thinking
Law of the Lid
Wrong Soil
Ignoring Your Weaknesses

**Chapter 4** **Our Gifts and Potential** ................................ **55**

Everyone Has a Gift

**Chapter 5** **Essential Qualities of Successful Leaders** .. **63**

Integrity
Vision and Passion
Curious and Daring

**Chapter 6** **Essential Disciplines for Effective Leadership** ............... **81**

Organization
Time Management
Other Essential Disciplines

**Chapter 7** **Breaking Through to Effective Leadership** .................. **101**

**Conclusion** ................................................................ **107**

# INTRODUCTION

God has put a wealth of instruction about leadership in the Word of God. This knowledge has been put there so that we can really learn God's ways of doing things. The Bible says, **"Seek ye first the Kingdom of God and His righteousness and all these things shall be added unto you" [Matthew 6:33].** The *Amplified Bible* translates "seek ye first the Kingdom of God and His righteousness" as *"God's way of doing and being right."*

God's ways for becoming an effective leader are demonstrated throughout the Bible, especially in the story of Joseph in the Book of Genesis. The story of Joseph, the young dreamer who God raised up to save a nation from seven years of famine, is an excellent teaching on how God prepares a person for leadership. Leaders are born, but they must be developed. God illustrates this truth in the life of Joseph.

In these turbulent times of terrorist attacks, corporate scandals, economic recession, and eroding public confidence in government and those in authority, I believe there has never been a greater need for effective leaders operating under the anointing of God. In the following pages of this book, you will learn the principles of effective leadership. I have studied for many years the great leaders of the Bible—Joseph, the Apostle Paul, Daniel, and of course, Jesus Christ, the greatest leader of all. What I have studied I have applied in my own life, and I know it is the reason why God has blessed me so greatly in the ministry. Effective leadership is more than following a ten-step formula for success. Learning from these anointed men of God, who walked with God and followed His leading (over human logic and reasoning) will impart to you the "spirit" of leadership, if you're open to receive.

My prayer is that *The Spirit of Leadership* will greatly bless you and inspire you to diligently pursue a higher level of personal leadership so that you can fulfill your God-given destiny.

# Chapter One

# Dream

# CHAPTER ONE

## *LEADERSHIP BEGINS WITH A DREAM*

Let's review Genesis, chapter 37, because it says in Hosea 4:6 that "My people are destroyed for lack of knowledge."

> **"And Jacob dwelt in the land wherein his father was a stranger, in the land of Canaan."** [You know Canaan was the promised land.] **"These are the generations of Jacob. Joseph, being seventeen years old, was feeding the flock with his brethren; and the lad was with the sons of Bilhah, and with the sons of Zilpah, his father's wives: and Joseph brought unto his father their evil report. Now Israel loved Joseph more than all his children..." [Genesis 37:1-3a]**

Now, I want you to see where he started in verse 1 as "Jacob." Then, in verse 3, God calls him "Israel." Now how did Jacob get to be Israel? Can you remember what incident took place that got his name changed? Back in Genesis 32:24, Jacob had wrestled with an angel, and then in verse 28 God says, *"Thy name shall be called no more Jacob, but Israel."* Jacob means "trickster," "deceiver," and "supplanter." However, Israel refers to "ruling with God." So, now you see that this change took place as Jacob struggled or wrestled with an angel.

Let's go back to Genesis 37. It says in verses 3-8:

**"Now Israel loved Joseph more than all his children, because he was the son of his old age: and he made him a coat of many colours. And when his brethren saw that their father loved him, more than all his brethren, they hated him, and could not speak peaceably unto him. And Joseph dreamed a dream, and he told it [to] his brethren: and they hated him yet the more. And he said unto them, 'Hear, I pray you, this dream which I have dreamed: For, behold, we were binding sheaves in the field, and, lo, my sheaf arose, and also stood upright; and, behold, your sheaves stood round about, and made obeisance to my sheaf.' And his brethren said to him, 'Shalt thou indeed reign over us? or shalt thou indeed have dominion over us?' And they hated him yet the more for his dreams, and for his words."**

Now, Joseph told the dream, and when he told

the dream, that is when it looked like everything began to fall in on him because his brethren hated it. They hated the fact that he had the dream, and they hated the fact that he told them about the dream. Then they hated him for what the dream was about. So now in verses 9-10:

> **"And he dreamed yet another dream, and told it (to) his brethren, and said, 'Behold, I have dreamed a dream more; and, behold, the sun and the moon and the eleven stars made obeisance to me.' And he told it to his father, and to his brethren: and his father rebuked him, and said unto him, 'What is this dream that thou hast dreamed?'"**

I want to highlight ***"What is this dream that thou hast dreamed?"*** because this is where we start in terms of leadership. What God is doing now is preparing Joseph for leadership. As you can see, one of the first things Joseph had to have was a dream. He had to see something that other people couldn't see. Therefore, if we are going to become an effective leader, we are going to have to dream. God has made

*If we are going to become an effective leader, we are going to have to dream.*

it so that everyone can dream. It's not so much that God singled out one man, Joseph, and just let him have a dream, but we are all capable of dreaming. In fact, Satan is a dream stealer. He will try to steal a dream and turn it into a nightmare. What we want to do is come back to the dreams that God has given us because inside of that dream lies our purpose, and inside that purpose lies our potential.

As we look at this dream that Joseph dreamed and then told to his brethren, his brethren got jealous. Now let's look at Matthew 15:12:

> **"Then came His [Jesus'] disciples, and said unto him, 'Knowest thou that the Pharisees were offended, after they heard this saying?'"** [Here's another group that's taken offense.] **"But He answered and said, 'Every plant, which my heavenly Father hath not planted, shall be rooted up. Let them alone: they be blind leaders of the blind. And if the blind lead the blind, both shall fall into the ditch.'" [Matthew 15:12-14]**

Isn't this interesting? You can have leaders who are blind. They have no vision. Let's go to Proverbs 29:18 where it says, **"Where there is no vision, the people perish [or are destroyed] . . ."** So many times and you see cities, communities, families, churches that seem to be destroyed, or not growing; or people fighting among people; or just a lot of things going on that are destructive, usually it is because of a lack of vision. Something has happened to the vision of the leadership. Now what God wants to do is to get the right leadership back in there.

Let's go to Acts 26. The Apostle Paul had an experience on the Damascus road. There was a light brighter than the noonday sun that struck Paul as he was riding on the road to Damascus. As you know, he was on his way to get Christians, to arrest them, because he thought they were Jews that had gone after some strange doctrine, but God got a hold of him. Then Paul explained to King Agrippa that God spoke to him:

> **"And when we were all fallen to the earth, I heard a voice speaking unto me, and saying in the Hebrew tongue, 'Saul, Saul, why persecutest thou me? it is hard for thee to kick against the pricks.' And I said, 'Who art thou, Lord?' And He said, 'I am Jesus whom thou persecutest. But rise, and stand upon thy feet: for I have appeared unto thee for this purpose,** [Notice, there's a purpose.] **to make thee a minister and a**

**witness both of these things which thou hast seen, and of those things in the which I will appear unto thee; Delivering thee from the people, and from the Gentiles, unto whom now I send thee, To open their eyes, and to turn them from darkness to light, and from the power of satan unto God, that they may receive forgiveness of sins, and inheritance among them which are sanctified by faith that is in me.'" [Acts 26:14-18]**

This is Paul and his calling. Paul was called to the Gentiles. He was not called to take the Word to the Jews. Well, you would have thought God would have called him to take the word to the Jews because Paul was brilliant. He studied under Gamaliel. He was a Pharisee among Pharisees. He had all of this knowledge. They tell me that he naturally was a brilliant man. You would think that he would have been called to the Jews—to his people—but God didn't send him there. God sent a man who was cussing, named Peter. God sent Peter to the Jews and He sent Paul to the Gentiles.

Verse 19 states, **"Whereupon, O king Agrippa, I was not disobedient unto the heavenly vision."** There can be a vision from God, but the enemy will try to give visions as well. The enemy will try to get people to see their cars being stolen. Satan will try to get people to see themselves starting a gambling casino. Understand, they can move into leadership, but it's not God's vision. It's not God's vision for a man to see himself selling cocaine. Yet, you've got leaders who are in that area of doing wrong things. It's not a heavenly vision.

Now when God gives us a calling or gives us a vision, He takes us through a series of steps to be able to perfect it, because inside of that vision lies our gifts. I want to show you two things. In Galatians 1:11-12, **"But I certify you, brethren, that the gospel which was preached of me is not after man. For I neither received it of man, neither was I taught it, but by the revelation of Jesus Christ."**

Now look at verse 15, **"But when it pleased God, who separated me from my mother's womb, and called me by His grace, to reveal His Son in me, that I might preach Him among the heathen; immediately I conferred not with flesh and blood" [Galatians 1:15-16].** Once Paul received the call from God to take the gospel to the Gentiles, Paul didn't ask his flesh, or consult his denomination, or go back to ask his mind and traditional thinking what it thought about it. He moved out based on a revelation from God.

As you know, the Apostle Paul is responsible for writing most of the *New Covenant or Testament.* Here was a man who couldn't even ask anybody what they thought about him taking the Word to the Gentiles. He had to do exactly what God had called him to do. It's interesting because when God gives you a vision, some people who don't mean any harm will sometimes try to come against you.

I, along with other men and women of God, recently received a permit from the federal regulators to open a full-service commercial bank called "New Covenant Community Bank." This bank is now only in one location, however, we plan to open other branches all over the world. I've traveled to many countries and have found that if you want money wire transferred to some of them, it is tough to do. There are so many rip-off artists and money gets held up and the officials claim they don't know where it is. However, if you had your own bank in some of these countries, you wouldn't have to fight with some of those demons of the world.

A fairly well–known person had come to my office and I asked him about starting a bank. He said, "No, don't do that" and so forth. Well, at that point in time, I could have been very discouraged and said, "Maybe I heard the wrong thing. Maybe that wasn't God at all." But I know God's voice. I received it and I moved forward.

Now, when I moved forward, God began to move, and He sent me a bank president who had been in banking for 30 years, a strong Christian. He came to me because it just so happened that he had some issues with a bank where he was previously the president. When we met, I said, "Listen, God has been speaking to me about a bank." I told him, "Pray about it and maybe we can get together and do something." He prayed about it and came back a couple weeks later and the next thing you know we teamed up together. We went to the federal regulators and had to put together all kinds of documents. It took us about eight months to get that done, but the regulators approved it.

We have now opened the bank to the Body of Christ, and the public, through a public stock offering so they can buy the stock to own the bank. With this bank, we can now make investments that are consistent with the values for a good quality of life. When you put your money in a regular bank, the bank will normally make the investments and do what it takes to get a return on their money. All of which is not consistent with a godly lifestyle. If we really believe there's going to be a wealth transfer and large amounts of wealth are coming into the Body of Christ, then where are you going to put it? Certainly not right back where it was before. That doesn't make sense.

I've discovered that people who really have a revelation of things to come will prepare. Noah was called by God. God called Noah and told him it was going to flood and to build an ark. It's interesting as to what happens when you really have a revelation. You can see something that other people can't see. You'll start acting differently than other people act.

I was at a ministers' meeting and a man of God got up and he spoke a word. He said, "Bill Winston, let me tell you that God told me to tell you that bank He gave you is from heaven. Don't let the devil steal it." The man who told me that is a well–known prophet of God. What God has given you may be unlike anything that has been heard of or done before. That doesn't matter. Don't allow dream stealers to steal what God has given you.

## Key Points

- Leadership starts with a dream or a vision.
- People without a Vision may discourage you because they cannot see what you see.
- Revelation will cause you to see what other people can't see.
- What God has given you may be unlike anything that has been heard of or done before.
- Don't let the dream stealers steal what God has given you.

# Chapter Two

# Leader

# CHAPTER TWO

## *WHAT IS A LEADER?*

**"And his master saw that the Lord was with him, and that the Lord made all that he did to prosper in his hand. And Joseph found grace in his sight, and he served him: and he made him overseer over his house, and all that he had he put into his hand." [Genesis 39:3-4]**

It seems that wherever Joseph went, he ended up being in charge of everything. People saw something in Joseph that made them want to put him in charge—in leadership.

What is a leader? ***A leader is one who guides by influence, or one who directs by going before, or along with.***[1] Notice I said, *"guides by influence."* It means you should have yourself so together until people want to be like you. You should have yourself to the point that people want to follow where you're going and not be forced to march.

I'm talking about influencing others. When I

was a little boy in the second or third grade, I had a sweetheart named Denise who was in my class. She was the daughter of a man who was one of the most well–known African–American fighter pilots in the world. The Tuskegee Airmen came out of Tuskegee, Alabama where I grew up. When I was very small, that was the only military base where they were training African–American pilots, and Denise's father was one of them. He had superior skills in flying and went on to be a General.

Denise's father would go overseas, and when he would come back, he would sometimes come to the school to pick up his daughter with his uniform on. I would see that uniform and I would say, "I'm going to be like that when I grow up." When I later went to college, I suddenly had a strong desire to be a fighter pilot. What had been planted in me was an image, or a seed when I was very small. Her father never sat down to talk to me and say, "William, don't you want to fly?" He didn't have to say that, he was just there leading by influence.

The statement that he made in accomplishing what he did made an impact in my life. The next thing you know, it influenced me to go into the Air Force and fly. I went on and flew fighter jets for years, and I loved it. Therefore, people can come into your life and be an influence to you. Not because they hang around you so much, but because you see something in them, a mark that you want to hit. They can have an influence on your life that you will never forget, but it's a seed that is sown in your life. That's what a leader is, someone who leads by influence.

**Second, a leader is one who others want to follow.** Notice what I didn't say, "Who others are made to follow." Have you ever heard the expression, "Do as I say do and not as I do?" That's not a good leader. The best way to lead people is by example. People are watching your example and they want to follow you and not be made to follow you. I've worked at different places in my life and have noticed that even in corporations, leaders were put in certain positions and their subordinates knew that person was not a good leader. These subordinates were made to follow that leader, and that was never a good thing. It's not an ideal environment for people to develop their gifts, nor for people to have the freedom to maximize their potential.

**Next, a leader is also one who leads others to**

**leadership.** What Jesus was trying to do in His ministry for those three and half years was trying to develop leaders. He had with Him, for the most part, twelve disciples. Notice, He was developing them into leaders because if He could put what was in Him in the disciples, they could change the world. He had three and half years to do it. I'm going to talk about time management in a later chapter, but we can see here that **a leader must respect and manage time to accomplish their calling or vision.** If you're not going to manage your time, you're not going to be effective as a leader, and you'll find that you'll never prosper in the way God wants you to prosper.

Jesus was able to do a whole lot in a very short period of time. He was trying to train the disciples because the proof of them being trained is that He could leave. A job of leaders is not to make followers. That is a lie! A job of a leader is to make leaders. People who are bound by an inferiority complex have a hard time making leaders because they quickly feel too intimidated. They think somebody is going to take their job. As a pastor, for example, it's not so much that the people I have now are trained to take over as pastor in our church, but that they are trained as leaders to be able to go out and start other churches, if called by God. They can separate from the pastor. That's the key. If you can't separate from the leader, something is wrong with that leadership–if you're making leaders for that purpose. You should be able to make decisions on your own at some point in time. There are people raising children who have a boy, 35 years old, that they are still trying to get him to make up his bed and they are begging him, "Why don't you get up and get a job?" You need to put the boy out! Change the locks on the door and don't even let him come back home!

Finally, **a leader is one who possesses character and inspires confidence.** Sometimes we think that character and confidence should be separated and that's not true. As a leader, your private life is just as important as your public life. You can't live one way publicly, and then privately you are another person. That is called duplicity. That will not work. It will confuse your children and everyone else.

*As a leader, your private life is just as important as your public life.*

When we were growing up, there was never a real difference between the adult and the teenager. The teenager was an aspiring adult. The further you go back in history, the closer the teenager was to imitating their mother or father. But today, they have created a sub-culture through music and so forth. And that's why we're having such a problem in getting young people to transition into leaders because the gap is getting bigger. I hope you're following me on this. I know that young people are young and they are learning things, however, they were never as wild as they are today.

When I was a young boy, I had come in from the barber one time and my father asked me, "Did you tell him to take it all off?" I said, "No, I didn't tell him to take it all off." My father would make me go back and tell him to take it all off. I'm only saying that today there's a gap and because of it, it's creating a leadership void. It's almost like people expect for their teenagers to run wild. That's a lie! That's a trick of the enemy because he's trying to stop leadership.

I've been working since the age of thirteen. I remember the time when I was about fourteen and there was a block party outside of my house. This guy I knew named Bud Arnold had a truck, and I jumped in his truck and started it up. I was going to put it in gear and drive off. Well, I didn't know it, but I had the gear in reverse, and I hit the accelerator. Boom! I hit our next door neighbor's car. My Lord! I went in the house and told my daddy. He said to me, "Son, you are going to have to pay for that. And all your checks for four months are going to come to me." I was held responsible.

Something is happening to leadership. This is all I'm saying. I'm not trying to come down on someone's freedom, but folks, there is a spirit of rebellion. It's a spirit, and it will have you dress a certain way, talk a certain way, listen to certain music, and so forth. I couldn't bring that stuff in the house. Look at the programming that's being shown on TV now, and tell me if that could have been aired 20 or 30 years ago. You couldn't show that stuff on TV. If somebody heard or saw that, they would shut the whole network down. But the spirit that has come in the world is having people to accept mediocrity.

I have to work with my son. I have told him that he can't wear certain clothes. He'll tell me, "Dad, I'm working and making my own money." And I'll tell him again, "You ain't wearing that." Some parents are intimidated, but you can't be because you are the leader that they are looking for. Do you realize that people want to do right? That's why we have our men's meetings at our church. Why? The men need to come together. The men in the household are to guide the home and guard it against evil. True, there's nothing like a mother's love. The mother would say, "Oh, he's alright." My dad would say, "He's not alright! Bring the boy in here, and let's deal with it." I'm saying there are two sides. God is merciful, but God is also just.

In leadership, competence and character run together. Now it's hard to find a good dentist, or a good doctor because it's all being dumbed down by the evil forces of this world. Stephen Covey shares the following example which brings out this point[2]. Let's say that you needed an operation and I posed this question to you. "Which doctor would you rather go to?" Here's a surgeon, and ninety percent of his surgeries are successful. But, he lies on the insurance forms, he is not being faithful to his wife, he doesn't go to church, and he doesn't care about God. Now you may go to another doctor who is a Bible-toting, foot stomping, Hammond organ–dancing Believer, but, he has lost fifty percent of his patients. Now if you had to have some surgery, and I told you all this, which doctor would you choose? Probably the first doctor because he has competence. The second doctor has character.

The problem has been that when you come into church, all of a sudden the standards go way down. Somehow people don't think they have to have their skills developed and sharpened, and so forth. Many times people who have high standards don't want to come in the church because they say folks are hiding from reality and don't really want to go anywhere and be anything. They say we want to stay in the church and praise the Lord all day. Please understand what I'm saying here because it was always meant that the Word become flesh. That means what you get in church, you are suppose to live out there.

This is the message that people are waiting on. When they see people who are raised to high positions and are excellent at what they do, and see that they are Christians at the same time, they will want to know who your God is. I got so many people saved at IBM. Here I was at the top of the ladder in sales in Chicago, and at the same time I was serving God. Boy, I would bring 5 to 6 people to church every Sunday to get them saved, and I was in management. I'm just saying look at what can happen. Somehow we've decided that if we serve God, that's good enough. No! When you serve God, you ought to take care of the things in your life that would make a statement in the world.

I would go to seminars at places like Northwestern University, but they were not talking about Christianity. They would talk about how executives can get more productivity out of their balance sheets. I would say, "I'm going to take that little course." And, I'm in there, however, I am saying that in our lives let us bring them both together. Let's make it so that we not only have them praising the Lord, but we aren't killing everybody on the operating table!

In short, effective leaders are people who influence others by example, and not by force. They are people of character, competence, and excellence who inspire others to be like them. They know a big part of their mission is to develop others as leaders.

## KEY POINTS

- A true leader guides by influence and not by force.
- Your accomplishments can sow the seeds to inspire leadership in others.
- Effective leaders must manage their time.
- Effective leaders will develop other leaders who can readily separate and go out on their own.
- As a leader, your private life is just as important as your public life.
- The current teenage sub-culture makes it difficult for our youth to transition into leadership.
- Character and competence are both required in good leaders.
- The Church should have higher standards of excellence than the world.
- Effective leaders know a big part of their mission is to develop other leaders.

# *Chapter Three*

# *Barriers*

# CHAPTER THREE

## *BARRIERS TO EFFECTIVE LEADERSHIP*

One reason why many people don't get what God has given them is because they are too intimidated and they have "boxed thinking." For Joseph to accomplish the dream that God had given him, he had to get out of the box.

A second reason, or barrier, that stops people from effective leadership and fulfilling God's calling is being in the wrong soil. Many times God wants to move people from where they are to a new place so that their gifts and potential can be maximized. Unfortunately, though, many people refuse to move.

Lastly, a third reason why some people fail to reach their God-given destiny is because they ignore their weaknesses. Many aspiring and established leaders have fallen because they refused to attack their weaknesses and satan used their weaknesses to destroy them or to make them ineffective.

## Boxed Thinking

Let's look at the first reason I mentioned "boxed thinking." Dr. I.V. Hilliard teaches this concept,[3] and his illustration will add clarity to this section on "Barriers to Effective Leadership." All right, here's a box. Now satan's job is to keep you in there. His job is also to keep you from the full expression of potential that God has for your life. Now, one side of that box is called the **"comfort zone."** One of the main reasons why people don't obey God and are not the kinds of leaders that can move the Body of Christ forward is because of the "comfort zone." They would rather stay comfortable. But Jesus didn't come to make you comfortable, He came to make you conformable. He came to conform you into the image of Christ, not comfortable, because you know when you're being conformed, it's not comfortable.

Another side of that box is "**inferiority complex**." An "inferiority complex" involves a lot of different things for people. You don't have to be a certain color to have an "inferiority complex." It is feeling inferior as to how God made you. We are the righteousness of God. I am a child of God. I am the seed of Abraham. I am a Christian, which means the "anointed ones." I am not inferior to anybody. It doesn't make any difference who they are or what color they are. That doesn't intimidate me one iota because I know who I am in God. The "inferiority complex" can keep us inside of that boundary. People get afraid to express their real self, so they stay inside that box.

Another side of that box is "**fear of failing**." People do not launch out because they fear failure. Understand, they read the same Bible you read that says, ". . .**If God be for us, who can be against us?" [Romans 8:31].** It's the same Bible you read that says, God **"always causeth us to triumph..." [II Corinthians 2:14].** It's the same Bible we read where it says, **"There shall not any man be able to stand before thee all the days of thy life: as I was with Moses, so I will be with thee..." [Joshua 1:5].** And the same Bible that says, **"I will never leave thee, nor forsake thee [or let you down]" [Hebrews 13:5].** Now, these are covenant promises. There isn't anyone who can give you better promises than God. If God can't keep His Word, we are all in trouble.

What people do is they go around like chickens. They go around with perverse speech and entertain corrupt thoughts, and those thoughts come in and put a stronghold on their minds. Now for some reason they can't move. They are paralyzed. Fear is designed to paralyze you. The first thing that a poisonous snake does is bite its victim. It has to stop the victim from moving. The snake has to poison it first; it has to kill the victim. A boa snake constricts. It wraps itself around a person and chokes the life out of them. But this snake doesn't stop choking until it senses that all of the life is gone. Then the snake eats the victim.

The same thing happens with the devil. The first thing the devil has to do is stop you. So what the devil does is he tries to bite you with the poison called "fear." When you fear, you're being poisoned. If you fear dying, or the pain you are feeling in your chest, you're being poisoned. If you fear getting on an airplane, or fear that somebody won't like you, you're being poisoned. You'll see that you will start slowing down. Why? The vision that you had is now being sapped and it's slowly diminishing because fear has come in.

Fear will cut off that heavenly vision and cause you to be blind. I'm not talking about the eyes. Satan doesn't come to blind your eyes; he comes to blind your mind. Why? He knows you don't see with your eyes; you see with your mind. If you blindfold somebody and then tell them to go across a room to a table in the back, you'll notice how slowly they move. Why? Because they are blind. Blindness stops your progress. What you have to do is come back and retrench, and get the fear out. Say aloud "No fear here." Whatever the fear is in your life, attack it. You have to replace it with faith, and **"faith cometh by hearing, and hearing by the Word of God" [Romans 10:17].** Attack it. It doesn't matter what it is.

*Fear will cut off that heavenly vision and now you're blind.*

You would be surprised at what people fear. Fear like, "I'm going to die like my mama." The enemy will just work you over. The first thing that happened to Adam when he fell in the garden is that he feared. When God came looking for him, the Bible says Adam said, **"I was afraid" [Genesis 3:10].** Why? Because faith perverted is fear. It's twisted. That's why Jesus called them a perverse generation. It's a twisted generation. So now we have got to get the fear out. That's the side of the box that's designed to keep you in there. The moment you step outside that box, fear hits.

Notice what fear did to the children of Israel when they came in and saw the giants. They came back with a little fear. The first thing they said is let us make us a new leader because this one is leading us into these giants, and we're going to be slaughtered **[Numbers 14:3-4]**. Now notice what fear did. It made them have poor judgment. Fear will affect your judgment. The very people who are sent to help you, you begin to judge them as hurting you; and that's with everybody. Try to pull somebody who is fearful out of something. The first thing they will do is fight you. We've got to get rid of the fear. Say it aloud again, "No fear here."

Now understand that all of this pertains to Joseph because he was being raised up by God as a leader. So for him to get there, he's going to have to get out of this box, because there was a box holding Joseph and the rest of them on one side or the other. The moment you try to go to one side, here comes the inferiority complex, "Ah, I can't go there. My hair doesn't look right." All of that is to keep you in a box.

The next side of that box is "**unrecognized resources.**" Let's get a working example of that. Turn to II Kings, chapter 6, and read what it says. This is where a man named Elisha was being surrounded by the Syrian army. The reason why is because he was giving the secrets away to Israel as to which way the Syrian army was going to attack Israel. After he had done that three or four times, the king of Syria got disgusted and said there's a traitor in my camp. Then one of his servants said, no, it is not a traitor but there is a prophet in Israel and he knows what you are saying in your bedchamber **[II Kings 6:11-13].** God was giving Israel secrets through the man of God. The Syrian king told his men to go get him.

The king sent a big host of soldiers to Dothan and surrounded it by night. They did it by night because in the daytime, Elisha might have seen them coming and escaped. The Syrian army didn't want Elisha to escape. But he didn't need to escape because he had "unrecognized resources." Then in the morning, the servant of the man of God, Gehazi, got up to get the man of God something. Gehazi went out there to do it, and when he looked up, he saw that they were surrounded by the Syrian army. Well, Gehazi panicked. Look what it says here in verse 15:

> **"And when the servant of the man of God was risen early, and gone forth, behold, an host compassed the city both with horses and chariots. And his**

> **servant said unto him, 'Alas, my master! how shall we do?' And he [Elisha] answered, 'Fear not: for they that be with us are more than they that be with them.'" [II Kings 6:15-16]**

Now I'm sure the man of God began to count in his mind, "one thousand, two thousand, three thousand. . .let me see, I'm trying to figure this out." The point is, one of them had understanding of "unrecognized resources." Verse 17 says, **"And Elisha prayed, and said, 'Lord, I pray thee, open his eyes, that he may see.' And the Lord opened the eyes of the young man; and he saw: and, behold, the mountain was full of horses and chariots of fire round about Elisha."**

Angels had surrounded the Syrian army; go to Hebrews 1:14 to find that when you get born-again, God assigns angels to you. All you have to do is go back to Psalm 34:7 to read that **"The angel of the Lord encampeth round about them that fear him (God), and delivereth them."** I don't know about you, but I fear God. That means that I have a reverential fear of God, not a terror-like fear. There is a difference. Don't you fear God? So you've got angels with you right now, however, those angels don't automatically move. Those angels move based on a command.

First, the man of God prayed, **"Lord, I pray thee, open his eyes."** This tells me that a secret to unrecognized resources is prayer. One of the things that the enemy tries to do is get you to negate your prayer life. Folks, I pray every morning. Normally, I pray every morning, about 99.9 percent of the time. Rarely, on an occasion, I may wait and pray later that day. Why? Because I've got to start in the spirit. I can't start in the flesh. I've got to start in the spirit because one of the things that takes you up is prayer. I pray in the spirit and in the natural. I have my own prayer book that I use. One book that you can use is called Prayers That Avail Much.[4] It has all kinds of prayers in it. Another one you can use is called Praying God's Word[5]. This is the book I used when I prayed for my wife. I thought she had the problem, but I found out it was mine.

Six months after we got married, I was having problems with my marriage because I felt I had married the wrong woman. Then I went to a meeting and a man said, "Start confessing God's Word over your spouse." Well, I came back and began to get into this book and I prayed:

> **Father, I thank you that I have a virtuous woman. She always does me good as long as there is life within her. The bread of idleness, gossip, discontent, and self-pity she will not eat. She will get up early and get spiritual food for the house. She assigns her maids their tasks, etc.**

The word is working mightily in our marriage. We've been transformed into the image of Jesus by the renewing of our minds.

I did that every day, and as I did, the image began to change. I found out what my problem was. I came from a house with a broken marriage when I was a child. I saw some things happen, some infidelity, and in my heart, I didn't trust women. I didn't find that out until I got into a pressured situation. When you get into pressure, you will find out what you really believe.

So what I believed was written back when I was a child, and it began to come up in my life. What it began to do was make me fear marriage. Now I tried to find a way to back out of it. Judgment took over, but it happened to be poor judgment because it was based on fear. The next thing that happened was I started confessing that prayer over my wife thinking it was going to change her. But who do you think it started changing? Right!. . .Me!

We have to pray for people. The Bible says in 1 Timothy 2:1-2 that we should pray for those in leadership. We have to pray for leaders because they are under attack. Why? Because we've been made to have leadership. Also, pray God's Word over other things such as: the Church, those in ministry, our nation, our families, etc.

I also pray in tongues. Why? Because "**He that speaketh in an unknown tongue edifieth himself**" **[1 Corinthians 14:4].** It takes you above the flesh realm. You can start seeing things that need to be seen. I do this everyday. I pray for my wife, my family, myself, my ministry, the businesses, etc. I don't back down on that because I know prayer is the thing that God needs so that He can do the work that I need Him to do in this earth.

So let's go back to II Kings 6. The prophet Elisha asked the Lord to open his servant's eyes, and God opened his eyes. Now, Gehazi's eyes were already opened—that's how he saw the Syrian army. What Elisha was saying when he prayed, **"Lord, I pray thee, open his eyes,"** was open his "spiritual eyes." So remember, you've got two sets of eyes, four eyes. You've got both spiritual eyes and natural eyes. Your natural eyes can't see but so far, but your spiritual eyes can see into the future or into the spiritual realm. When God opened Gehazi's eyes, he saw that the Syrian army was surrounded by angels. I'm talking about "unrecognized resources."

Now the next thing Elisha did is he **"prayed unto the Lord, and said, 'Smite this people, I pray thee, with blindness'" [II Kings 6:18]**. The angels with one swoop blinded every member in the army. That whole army came for one man, and this one man whipped an entire army. This goes to show you the ability that we have as Christians. If we know how to use the Covenant, nobody can stop you. Nobody can stop you from taking your city. Nobody can stop you from doing what God has called you to do. But we've got to realize there's a fear of failure, there's an inferiority complex, there's a comfort zone, and there are unrecognized resources that are set out to stop people.

## The Law of Lid

There's another hindrance that comes in to try to stop people from "effective leadership." If you got a box and you put something in it, you're going to put a lid on top of the box to make sure that what you put in it doesn't get out. This lid, or hindrance, is called the *"law of the lid"*, a concept taught by John Maxwell[6]. The law of the lid says that you will never go any further than your leader. This is the law of the lid. So for God to do something for Joseph, He couldn't leave him where he was. Joseph's brothers, at first, were going to kill him. They threw him down in a pit, and then they decided to sell him as a slave to the Ishmeelites who were heading down to Egypt. They bought Joseph as a slave and took him to Egypt. Understand, Joseph's brothers were jealous. His dad told him to stop his foolish talking, but God had put something in Joseph. Now all of a sudden, for Joseph to blossom, he's going to have to be taken from under that leadership. God had to take him to Egypt.

I am only saying this because sometimes God wants to move people. He wants to take somebody who may be in a certain community. You know some people may say, "This is our community and we want to stay in it." Maybe it's a certain school that you want to go to, but maybe God doesn't want you to go to that kind of school. Maybe He wants to take you up to Lewiston, Maine to

Bates College. Perhaps that is where you'll find the right leadership for Him to raise you up in the kind of vocation that will make you a leader for the world.

Even in a new place, some of you will look for the comfort zone. You go to class and you look around the classroom. You don't see but one other student from your country and you want to sit by that person. God may not want you to sit by that person. He may want you to sit by someone who is from Japan. When God starts moving people around like that, they sometimes get out of their comfort zone and they get fearful, and God can't do but so much with them and they end up never fulfilling their destiny. Oh, they may do a little something, but it's just a drop in the bucket as compared to what God wanted to do with them.

## The Wrong Soil

Closely related to the law of the lid is being in the wrong soil, the third barrier to developing as a successful leader. Now God is moving Joseph. And as He is doing this, He is taking Joseph from one place to another. And it so happens that Joseph ended up going in chains.

To illustrate the importance of being in the right place to develop as an effective leader, let's use the example of an acorn seed. Now an oak tree comes from the acorn seed. The oak tree is in that seed. To get the oak tree out of the seed, you must put the seed in some soil. The shell on the acorn seed, when it gets into proper soil, breaks open and the tree comes out. Now the seed has to get into proper soil for all of this to happen. Sometimes people can't flourish because they are not in proper soil.

The acorn seed represents your life because everything that you are to be is already in there. Every acorn seed has every limb, every branch, and every leaf already in that seed and nothing will be added to it. We've just got to get some soil, the right soil. Not only does the seed bring forth a tree, but inside of that tree is a forest. And inside of that forest is the lumber for your house. This is called ***potential.*** Potential can be defined as ***unused ability, hidden talent, reserved power, untapped strength, unused success.***

Somebody said the wealthiest place in the world is not the gold mines of South Africa, or the oil fields of Kuwait, but that the wealthiest place in the world is the graveyards. That's where all the potential is buried because the people never did anything with it.

## Ignoring Your Weaknesses

The final reason why many people fail to become effective leaders and complete what God has called them to do is because they ignore their weaknesses. It is sad to say, but we got folks who will tell you one thing and then do something different, or their life doesn't match their preaching, or for some reason they will get in places of high authority and do things they are not right. Their weaknesses prevent them from being a leader with integrity and the courage to obey God and do what is right.

I heard one man say this and I think it is just profound. Some people will say don't focus on your weakness. This man said that's not true. Where your focus should be in terms of you working and developing your life, <u>should</u> be on your weaknesses. Here's why this man says that...because your greatest weakness will keep you from reaching your greatest desire. What people tend to do is say, "Well, I have all these credits on my strength side, and everybody has some kind of weakness." Then they don't work on them.

*Your greatest weakness will keep you from reaching your greatest desire.*

Take the example of King David. He wanted to build a temple for God, but God didn't let him build it. God said, **"Thou shalt not build an house for my name, because thou hast been a man of war, and hast shed blood" [1 Chronicles 28:3]**. David slew many men in war, and was bloody because he had Uriah, the Hittite, killed because he wanted Uriah's wife, Bathsheba. Isn't that interesting? David's greatest desire was to build the temple. That was one of the things David was called to do. It was in God's plan, but what stopped David was his greatest weakness and that was lust. That was having to see women as people to be conquered.

You've got to work on your weakness. Don't push it off to the side because it will stop you from reaching your greatest desire. Work on it! Don't try to talk yourself out of it, thinking that it doesn't exist. It does exist. If your greatest weakness is in the area of giving money, in that for some reason tithing is still hard for you to do, you need to go to work on it because it will stop you from reaching your greatest desire. It can be worked on. God wouldn't tell you to work on it if it couldn't be worked on. What the enemy will do is try to give you a keg of powder with a hole in it, and as you journey on up in getting promoted, the enemy will wait until you get very visible. Then he will light it, and your sins will find you out. Everybody has got some kind of weakness. Work on it.

I'm talking about leadership. You want to be a successful leader. Dr. Myles Munroe recommends asking yourself a series of questions to stimulate your thinking and launch you into a quest for effective living so that you can get the quality and the best out of your life[7]. Ask yourself: **1) Who am I? 2) Where am I from?** I'm not talking about Lake Charles, Chicago, or Mississippi; that's your heritage. **3) Why am I here?** That's your purpose and meaning. **4) What can I do?** That's your capacity. **5) Where am I going?** That's your destiny.

## KEY POINTS

- We should aggressively attack the unseen barriers that hinder our thinking like leaders.
- Conforming to the high calling of leadership will push us out of our comfort zone.
- Seeing yourself as God sees you will overcome that inferiority complex.
- Knowing and receiving by faith God's covenant promises for your success will drive out the fear of failing.
- Train your Spirit Man to perceive the resources that God has already placed all around you.
- The unseen resources provided for your success are more powerful than the perceived obstacles that are seen.
- The Secret to engaging unrecognized resources is Prayer.
- When you get under pressure, you will find out what you really believe.
- Pray for those in leadership.
- God may move you to a different environment, out of your comfort zone, so He can develop your potential.
- Everything you are to become is already within you, in seed form.
- Dealing with your weaknesses will prevent them from potentially causing your downfall.
- Ask yourself penetrating questions to see if you are following the right path to get you to your appointed Destiny.

# Potential

# CHAPTER FOUR

## *OUR GIFTS AND POTENTIAL*

Let's return to the life of Joseph and how God was preparing him for leadership. When God moved Joseph to Egypt, Joseph was being transported to an environment that was going to give him the type of environment that he needed to maximize his potential. Now God knows what that is, you don't. The reason why you don't is because you didn't create yourself. Don't go back to folks who didn't make you to find out who you are because they don't know who they are. They didn't make you. As close as you are to your mama, she doesn't know who you are. She doesn't know what you can do. I mean she may have some idea, but I'm saying, in general, your Maker is the one who knows all about you.

Remember the illustration of the acorn seed in the earlier chapter? The acorn seed represents your life, and, like that seed, God has already placed in you all that you are to be. However, you have to be in the right soil, under the right leadership, and in your right purpose for the full expression of your gifts and potential.

Proverbs 17:8 says, **"A gift is as a precious stone in the eyes of him that hath it: whithersoever it turneth, it prospereth."** This means that everyone reading this book has a gift. Now, one of the things the enemy tries to do is either hide your gift or use your gift for his purpose, because he knows it is through your gift that you have dominion. That's a profound word. It says in this verse that a gift is like a precious stone...it could be a diamond. Either way you look at a diamond, it's sparkling, but in turning the gift, the verse says, **"whithersoever it turneth, it prospereth."** What that means is that once you have been given a gift and you begin to turn it or work it, then the more you work it, the more you prosper.

Somebody once said that if you find your gift and work it for ten years, you will be a millionaire. Now I'm talking about working your gift out of the box. I'm not talking about staying in the comfort zone. I'm talking about doing all of the things that I've just talked about in the previous chapters. When I teach about things, I build line upon line. You work your gift. One of the things that happened to Adam is that he was gifted by God, and the enemy came in to shut it down.

Let's look at Proverbs 18:16, ***"A man's gift maketh room for him, and bringeth him before great men."*** You can believe that when you work this gift, it's going to promote you. I know we can apply it to money as well, but let's keep it in the context that we have here. Let's look at Joseph's life again. We read in Genesis 39: 1-2:

> **"And Joseph was brought down to Egypt; and Potiphar, an officer of Pharaoh, captain of the guard, an Egyptian, bought him [Joseph] of the hands of the Ishmeelites, which had brought him down thither. And the Lord was with Joseph, and he was a prosperous man; and he was in the house of his master, the Egyptian."**

Now understand that Joseph's brothers were trying to shut him down. Sometimes people are jealous of other folks' gifts, and the one reason they are is that they don't realize they have a gift. You don't need to fight over one another's gift. Do you realize there are some people who want to be a dentist or a dental hygienist? They want to look into somebody's halitosis mouth and work with those rotten teeth. Do you realize somebody wants to be a physician or nurse's aide, and change somebody's bedpan? Do you realize somebody wants to have a garbage collecting business and collect your filthy, stinking garbage? But I've seen some people in the garbage business who end up making a whole lot of money. I've seen folks in the bedpan-changing business who really command a whole lot of money.

My point is that God gave us all gifts that are to work together to make a society. Some people don't want to be a dentist, so don't get on them because God made it so that they could be in the garbage business or be an architect. And sometimes we say, "He doesn't do much, he's in the garbage business," because society has told us to talk down about the garbage business and talk way up if you are the CEO of Time-Warner. However, God never saw it like that because in the Kingdom of God it is the only place where you can be a domestic maid and have a corporate jet at the airport. It's the only place where you can do that. It's what God called you to do. God has got it so that somebody wants to be a farmer, an electrician, or a plumber. You don't think so much of a plumber until your toilet stops up, and then that plumber becomes "El Shaddai." You know what I mean? You get the plumber on the phone, and when the plumber comes in, you say, "Oh, glory to God. Thank you, Jesus." You are so happy to see that plumber because he wanted to be a plumber.

God put it in us to want to be something. Don't try to force somebody to be something they are not meant to be. If you have an inkling of what they could be or should be in life, start praying for them, but let God ultimately direct their destiny. You know what I mean? Now when kids are small, the Bible says, "they are shot as an arrow," meaning that you give them some training and direction [Psalm 127:4]. My son, since he was a little boy, told me he wanted to be a heart surgeon, a cardiologist. That's all he's ever said. Well, how about a preacher? I know in our city, there's a pastor of a very sizeable church, a Bishop, who is also a practicing pediatrician. So don't tell me what God can't do. See, we're trying to box God in again. We're trying to keep God in the box and He's not. If you hang with God, He'll take you out of the box. So I know my son is going to preach, but he wants to be a doctor, too.

## KEY POINTS

- Whatever your gift is, the more you work it, the more you prosper.
- Because your gift is unique to you, as you develop it, you will contribute significantly in the part you play in society.
- Pray for your children, that they, too, will reach their God-ordained Destiny.

# Chapter Five

# Qualities

# CHAPTER FIVE

## *ESSENTIAL QUALITIES OF EFFECTIVE LEADERS*

In this chapter, I spend a great deal of time talking about one of the most important qualities of an effective leader, **integrity.** When I say integrity, I mean character, trust, to walk uprightly, and to be faithful.

In Genesis 39:4, it says:

> **"And Joseph found grace** [another word for "grace" is favor] **in his sight, and he served him; and he made him overseer over his house, and all that he had he put into his hand. And it came to pass from the time that he had made him overseer in his house, and over all that he had, that the Lord blessed the Egyptian's house for Joseph's sake; and the blessing of the Lord was upon all that he had in the house, and in the field." [Genesis 4:4-5]**

Now the Egyptian's house was blessed because of Joseph. The blessings were on Joseph. So when the blessings are on you, and you work for someone, they, too, will be blessed. Verse 6 says, **"And he left all that he had in Joseph's hand. . ."** Now the scriptures keep saying that. So one of the things it is probably talking about is integrity. Notice the verse says, **"he left all that he [Potiphar] had**." Potiphar didn't even count it. He just trusted Joseph with his integrity. This is not the first time integrity is mentioned in the scriptures.

Let's go back to a couple of places and see what God refers to in talking about integrity. Let's look at Genesis 17:1, **"And when Abram was ninety years old and nine, the Lord appeared to Abram, and said unto him, I am the Almighty God [El Shaddai]."** Now, the "Almighty God" means the Breasty-One; that is, He can supply everything that you need in abundance. It also means the God who can override natural law. God is about to reset Abraham's body and Sarah's body because they were beyond the age of childbearing. So He is El Shaddai. He can start time, stop time, speed time up, or slow time down because He made time. When He said, "Let there be light," then the morning and the evening were the first day. Notice, there was time inserted in the earth because in the spirit there is no time.

That's why when you pray, you believe you received because the moment you pray, there's no time in the spirit. It's done. Now the only time is in the three-dimensional world in which you live. So with faith and patience you have to inherit the promise. That's why you've got to believe you receive when you pray, and just stand on that because it has happened.

Notice what it says in verse 1, **"...I am the Almighty God; walk before me, and be thou perfect."** The word *"perfect"* has to do with the integrity of God, upright, having integrity, or having character. God really brings it out in Genesis 20:1:

> **"And Abraham journeyed from thence toward the south country, and dwelled between Kadesh and Shur, and sojourned in Gerar. And Abraham said of Sarah his wife, She is my sister: and Abimelech king of Gerar sent, and took Sarah." [Genesis 20:1-2]**

So the king took Sarah into his harem.

> **"But God came to Abimelech in a dream by night, and said to him, 'Behold, thou art but a dead man, for the woman which thou hast taken; for she is a man's wife.' But Abimelech**

> **had not come near her: and he said, 'Lord, wilt thou slay also a righteous nation? Said he not unto me, She is my sister? And she, even she herself said, He is my brother: in the integrity of my heart and innocency of my hands have I done this.'" [Genesis 20:3-5]**

Abimelech is saying that he didn't know; he did it honestly. Now look at verse 6, **"And God said unto him in a dream, 'Yea, I know that thou didst this in the integrity of thy heart; for I also withheld thee from sinning against me: therefore suffered I thee not to touch her."** God is saying what kept Abimelech from sinning was his integrity. So integrity will keep you from sin.

A leader must have integrity. A leader never lies to other people and he never lies to himself. "First to thine ownself be true." You've got to be true to yourself. A leader must have trust. In other words, co-workers and others must trust you, like Potiphar trusted Joseph.

Let's look at a couple more places because integrity is all over the Bible. As a matter of fact, let's go over to the Book of Psalms. In Psalm 26:1, **"Judge me, O Lord; for I have walked in mine integrity. I**

**have trusted also in the Lord; therefore, I shall not slide."** Slide which way? Back. Integrity will keep you from backsliding.

Let's go to Proverbs 11:3, **"The integrity of the upright shall guide them: but the perverseness of transgressors shall destroy them."** So notice, by a person having integrity they can be guided by the Lord. Integrity will cause you to have right guidance.

Let's look at one more. Let's look at Proverbs 20:7, **"The just man walketh in his integrity: his children are blessed after him."** Notice, through a person walking in integrity, your children will be blessed.

All of this is telling you about integrity. For you to be a leader, God expects you to have integrity. This integrity will help you discover your full potential because you can be guided by God into the exact purpose that God has for your life. Just be full of integrity.

Integrity has to do with what you are on the inside. What you are on the inside, if given enough time, enough pressure, or right conditions, will eventually come out. So, what you want to do is go after that rascal. I mean all of us have something. I have to make myself go to the dentist because as a little boy, I remember sitting in the dentist's chair crying. So the experience of that got written on the inside, and I found myself putting it off. Your teeth are a very important part of your body.

So, in Genesis 39:6, it says:

> **"And he [Potiphar] left all that he had in Joseph's hand; and he knew not ought he had, save the bread which he did eat. And Joseph was a goodly person, and well favoured. And it came to pass after these things, that his master's wife cast her eyes upon Joseph; and she said, 'Lie with me.'" [Genesis 39:6-7]**

Now we're about to see what's inside of Joseph. The enemy tries to come with temptation as you, as a leader, are being promoted and developed. The temptation may be to take the glory from God, or to take some money that doesn't belong to you—that's the same thing as cheating on your income tax, or the temptation to do hair and not report it. I can go on. In every area, you've got to clean it up. Joseph didn't take anything that didn't belong to him because he was a steward. Part of your job as a leader in the earth is to be a steward. You have to manage things that don't belong to you, but you have to treat them as if you are responsible for bringing them back to the master with increase.

So, "lie with me" was sexual temptation. It could be that a pastor is in the pulpit and is tempted not to tell the people the truth because if he did, the denomination would take his papers back. That's where the enemy has been controlling the church for years. Well, what are you going to do? Side with the devil or side with God? Life is a series of decisions. And they don't stop because you made one good decision. On the other side of that decision, there is another decision. One of the things that keeps you from sinning is integrity, and the other is vision.

**Vision, coupled with passion,** is an essential quality of any successful leader. What keeps me getting up in the morning is vision. I've got too much at stake now. We've got a bank, a shopping mall, over 13,000 people in our church (and that's doubling this year), television, my kids, family, people who respect me. I've got a lot on the line here. The enemy knows that if he can get the leadership, then he can do great damage. Don't think the devil doesn't tempt somebody like me. As long as he knows that flesh is hanging on your body, he knows you can be tempted. I've got passion and I've got vision, but I don't have time for that. I've got to move on. I've got to get the job done here. Jesus may come back tonight, and if He comes back and finds somebody in someone else's bed... that's not right.

I'm only saying that because here is Joseph who was vulnerable. He was a young man. He was moving up the ranks. Sometimes when you're moving up the ranks, the old folks used to say you start smelling yourself. That pride will come just before a fall. You have to keep yourself humbly before the Word. If you follow the Holy Ghost, He'll keep you humble. Sometimes people try to humble you, but God is the one who does that. Just follow His Word and He'll keep you in a place of Bible humility.

So now Potiphar's wife comes to Joseph and tries to get him to lie with her. You know she was sent by the devil. She told Joseph that the master is away right now, and everything is right, nobody will see it. You're on a trip and nobody is going to see what you're watching on TV...just go ahead. Now I know I'm stepping on some toes, but we must develop leadership. So Joseph refused her. In verse 9 it says, **"There is none greater in this house than I; neither hath he [Potiphar] kept back any thing from me but thee, because thou art his wife: how then can I do this great wickedness, and sin against God?"** Joseph didn't say sin against the wife or Potiphar, because it didn't have anything do with them. God is everywhere. If you keep that in mind, that God is everywhere, you can always keep His presence with you and it'll mean so much to you.

Potiphar's wife came after Joseph again, and pressed him, and so forth, just like the devil will try to do sometimes. The wife snatched Joseph's garment, and he pleaded, and the next thing that happened, he was falsely accused by the wife. As a leader, you can be accused falsely. Jesus was accused falsely. If you look at all these things, Jesus was tempted in all His ways, yet He never sinned.

Turn to I Peter 4:12, **"Beloved, think it not strange concerning the fiery trial which is to try you, as though some strange thing happened unto you: But rejoice, inasmuch as ye are partakers of**

**Christ's sufferings... "** Now some people have interpreted that to be that Jesus suffered sickness and that's why we're going to have to suffer sickness, too. That doesn't mean that. It means partake. It means that because He took it, you don't have to. It means because He bore it, you can resist it. That's how you partake in His suffering. The flesh hates it when you side with the Word. It would rather lay down than resist the devil's attacks.

Look at what it says here in verse 13, **"...His glory shall be revealed, ye may be glad also with exceeding joy."** [So in that partaking, His glory will be revealed.] **"If ye be reproached for the name of Christ, happy are ye; for the spirit of glory and of God resteth upon you: on their part he is evil spoken of, but on your part he is glorified. But let none of you suffer as a murderer, or as a thief,** [Stealing something from the job.] **or as an evildoer, or as a busybody in other men's matters" [I Peter 4:14-15].** Now the Bible will straighten you out. Like I said, all you have to do is follow God's Word and it will keep you humble.

So, effective leaders must have a sense of purpose because in that purpose is a potential, and timing, and so forth. There has to be clear guiding vision in your life. It makes you persistent. It makes you get up in the morning. It makes you resist sin. As mentioned earlier, a leader also has to have passion. A leader must love what they are doing. Most folks are going to a job they can't stand and the reason why is because it's not in their gift. So they are doing it because they think that's the way they are going to make some money. They don't know that if they just crack into that gift, no matter what it is, whether it's being an artist, or musician, or whatever, that God is going to bless them in that gift.

The last thing a leader must have is **curiosity and daring**. When I say that, a leader must be willing to take risks—to step out in faith. A lot of people are not willing to do that and, as a result, they stay where they are and don't give themselves a chance to excel.

So these are the essential qualities of a leader. Let's finish up with Joseph. Look again at Genesis 39:20:

> **"And Joseph's master took him, and put him into the prison, a place where the king's prisoners were bound: and he was there in the prison. But the**

**Lord was with Joseph, and shewed him mercy, and gave him favour in the sight of the keeper of the prison. And the keeper of the prison committed to Joseph's hand all the prisoners that were in the prison; and whatsoever they did there, he was the doer of it. The keeper of the prison looked not to any thing that was under his hand; because the Lord was with him, and that which he did, the Lord made it to prosper." [Genesis 39:20-23]**

So now this is kind of interesting. Here is Joseph in prison, and what happened was that the butler and the baker made Pharaoh mad. Pharaoh threw them in prison and they ended up with Joseph. They woke up one day and they had this look on their faces. In Genesis 40:6, **"And Joseph came in unto them in the morning, and looked upon them, and, behold, they were sad. And he asked Pharaoh's officers that were with him in the ward of his lord's house, saying, 'Wherefore look ye so sadly to day?'" [Genesis 40:6-7].**

Now this might be a very, very, very simple verse to you. And you might be thinking, "Now there's nothing in that." Yes, there is. Joseph saw on their faces that they were sad. You may have expected that

Joseph's disposition was that he, too, was sad. If Joseph was sad, he wouldn't ask them that because misery loves company. In the lowest place in your life, you should still have joy. To not have joy is under the curse. It's a curse to be sad. It's a curse to have a sad countenance. I'm not saying to go around skinning and grinning at everybody,but I'm saying that for you to have a joyful countenance is a witness and that no matter what state I am in, I have joy.

What happens with a countenance any different from joy is that many times like when you have to go before the king? The kind of countenance you have to have is joy. Like Nehemiah, as the king's cupbearer, he had to have a joyful countenance or else he would have been killed. The king would not allow you to come before him and draw attention to yourself. And that's the same thing about the King you're standing before right now, right now, right now–while reading this book. Don't think because you can't see Him that He is not here. He is sitting here right now. He is watching our countenance. Depression is a problem of a person focusing in on himself or herself. That's why depression reigns. Get them outside of themselves and depression will leave just like that. That's what some people want to do is to draw attention to themselves.

They'll look sad and want someone to say, "What's wrong with you?" However, the king won't ask you that, he'll cut your head off.

Before closing this chapter, I have one more comment about trust. If people trust you, they will help you and possibly give you information vital to your success. Also, they may give you confidential information that they didn't tell anybody else. They will give it to you because maybe God led them to you because you have a wisdom flowing through you that could help them solve their problem. My point is that they didn't tell you for you to go out and tell other people about it. This would be a breach of trust and Joseph didn't have that. He kept Potiphar's business between he and Potiphar. Joseph did not tell Potiphar what his wife did. He didn't do it. The Bible says that a man is blessed who covers another man's sin, but we want to run out and tell everybody how somebody is falling short. We're quick to tell it. That keeps you from leadership. God can't trust you because you're trying to make someone else look bad so you can look good.

We were all born leaders. There's a gift in every one of us, but we still have to be developed. The purpose of this book is for leadership development, and continuous development. Even some of the highest CEOs go to seminars and sit through sessions to continue to develop themselves.

## KEY POINTS

- A Leader must have Integrity.
- Your Integrity will promote you and protect you from falling.
- Your Integrity will help you discover your full potential because you can be guided by God into the exact purpose that God has for your life.
- What you are on the inside, if given enough time, enough pressure, or right conditions, will eventually come out.
- Life is a series of decisions - A *good* Life is the result of a series of *good* decisions
- Maintaining a clear Vision will motivate you to get up in the morning.
- The further up you rise, the more important it is to maintain your Integrity for others' sake.
- You walk in Integrity all the time not because men see you, but because God sees you.
- A Leader must love what they are doing.
- A Leader must be willing to take risks - to step out in faith.
- A Leader chooses his disposition, and doesn't let circumstances pull him down.
- Leadership development is a continuous process.

# Chapter Six

# Disciplines

# CHAPTER SIX

## *ESSENTIAL DISCIPLINES FOR EFFECTIVE LEADERSHIP*

So let's go on. Joseph is in prison and it looks like everywhere he goes, he gets people to work with him. Obviously, Joseph had some organization skills because he was prospering Potiphar's house. True enough, God was working with him, but God needed something to work with. Joseph was put in prison and now it looks like he is organizing the prison.

Organization, structure, teamwork, and time management are essential disciplines in effective leadership. That is, to be effective as a leader, a person must be organized, know how to manage their time, and understand how to get work accomplished through others (delegation and teamwork) to achieve the mission.

In teaching about leadership at seminars, I often use the example of the structure and organization that exists on an aircraft carrier. In the military everything is by the book. Everyone knows their job, they are well trained in their jobs, and they work together as a team. Everyone is "mission-minded" so there is no strife or competition. In war, if people are not in their proper place or are not properly trained in their job, someone could lose their life. Everything is by the book.

On an aircraft carrier, there is an "Air Boss" who oversees everyone. His most important function is to ensure that people adhere to the standards that have been established and to successfully orchestrate the mission in a close environment. If people don't adhere to the standards, it could be hazardous. The "Air Boss" ensures the "effective readiness" of the team for wartime. The team's readiness or preparedness has one primary purpose: to defeat the enemy if and when the time comes. This is important to understand in ministry because, as the Church, we're not fighting people, we're fighting a spiritual war and we must be trained and ready to defeat our spiritual enemy.

What do you think about teamwork? True enough, we have different areas in the ministry or business which we are responsible for, but if there comes a time when a certain part of the ministry or business needs a thrust, then we might all converge on that project to make it happen and not grumble about it. For someone to say, "that's not my job," is not teamwork. The reason why strife was not present on the aircraft carriers I've been on is because everyone had a specific responsibility to carry out and everyone was mission-minded to get the job done safely and successfully. It seems like the mission overrides any strife or anything that would keep them from reaching their goal.

I've been in these environments. I was in combat in Southeast Asia. You don't know the difference over there between Sunday and Tuesday. You just fly—night and day. If you fly at night, you sleep during the day. If you fly in the day, you sleep at night. When you take off for a mission, the first thing you have to do is take off fully loaded because your target may be about four hundred miles north from where you are. You have to fill up with gas [fuel] to complete the mission, but you can't land to get it. You have to refuel in the air. You have to connect with a refueling tanker on the way to your destination because you're so heavily loaded and burning a lot of fuel. You need enough fuel so that after you hit the target, you'll have enough to return to base. So you've got to make sure that the tanker is where it should be.

There has to be people who are mission- minded, everyone working together and everybody in their place on time. Now I want you to think about this because I believe God is orchestrating something in the Earth and He is launching people with different assignments in the Body of Christ. He could be launching angels, or specific people to pray at a certain time. It's a combat zone we are in down here.

I remember times when new officers would come out for training in the combat zone. They would fly in the front seat as aircraft commander and I'd fly in the airplane with them. Although they were certified pilots and could fly, when they would try and hook up to the refueling tanker, the airplane was so heavy, and its center of gravity had shifted so much, that it caused the airplane to become much more difficult to control. I had to show them how to hook up to that tanker, and after a few times of trying they could do it perfectly. Ultimately, teamwork got the job done.

What I am trying to say is that there is a lot of coordination and teamwork needed in the military as well as any organization. Everyone's part is vital and important. If you are going to have an organization, you must have goals that will produce certain

*There is a mission that God has for every one of us. We've got to make it happen...*

results.You can and must be organized as an individual and as a team. We're all here for a certain reason in this earth. If you don't know why you're here, you need to find out. As quoted by Dr. Myles Munroe, "Where the purpose of a thing is not known, abuse [abnormal use] is inevitable"[7]. Go back in the Bible and find yourself in the book! There is a mission that God has for every one of us. We've got to make it happen and we cannot come back with negative results. We've got to accomplish what we've been gifted and placed in this earth at this time to do.

## ORGANIZATION

One of the key things a leader needs to possess for effective leadership is **organization.** Organization is simply defined as God's plan to simplify life. When you say organization, you're talking about putting something into working order. In business, it's the process of resource management. In the Bible, it's the gathering of all the elements or facts needed to accomplish that objective into a relationship that will produce the desired results. The Bible says a disorganized person will come to poverty. You can say "I believe I received," "I believe I'm a millionaire," but if you're disorganized, you will not get it because organization is a law. Mac Hammond says, "God will supernaturally add to your life as you are sufficiently organized to contain it."[8]

How organized are you? You're only as organized as you are in the unsupervised areas of your life. (Another gleaning from Dr. Hilliard.[3]) Look at your closet at home, the trunk of your car, that back-yard, etc. (If you can't say, "Amen," say, "Oh, me.") This is key because all of this is leadership development. You've got to be organized because if you're not, you will not produce the desired results.

For example, let's say I get a car engine and take it apart, and then someone tells me to put it back together again. I start putting it back together with some working plans. I try to start it, but it will not start. Although I've taken out all the parts that were given, it will not start. I then call an expert from the car dealership and they come in and tweak something here, turn something there, and so forth. They tell me to try it again, and the car starts rights up. What happened was, I didn't assemble the parts correctly and it didn't yield the desired result. I had all the parts, but they were out of order. The same can happen with a ministry or a business, etc. You can have people out of place or people in the right place, but not properly trained. Whether an employee or member of the armed services, it could produce results less than expected or desired.

Another word for organization in the Bible is "understanding." Understanding comes from a Hebrew word which means organization, **"with all thy getting get understanding"[Proverbs 4:7].** You can have all the parts, and all the knowledge, but if you don't understand it, you can't produce wisdom. So that's key. I'm saying this because Joseph was obviously organized. You can be well favored, but if you're truly organized, you will really excel.

Let's go to Proverbs 24:30-34.

> **"I went by the field of the slothful,** [A slothful person is lazy and a waster of time.] **and by the vineyard of the man void of understanding."** [Another word for understanding is organization.] **"And, lo, it was all grown over with thorns, and nettles had covered the face thereof, and the stone wall thereof was**

**broken down. Then I saw, and considered it well: I looked upon it, and received instruction. Yet a little sleep, a little slumber, a little folding of the hands to sleep: So shall thy poverty come as one that travelleth; and thy want as an armed man."**

What this is saying to me is that a person who is a time-waster and is disorganized will be held up like a bandit and robbed. If you go to anybody who is a time-waster, you can see how much they have in life. Go to the neighborhoods where they're hanging out on the corner. They are wasting time, and they are doing nothing. They are broke, and they will stay broke. Try to get an appointment with the Chairman of the Board at Sears-Roebuck, and see if you can get an appointment today. Do you think you will? No, because he is busy.

Now what happens is this. When you start making better use of your time, old friends will call you and you'll say, "Well, I've got to get some things done." And the person will say, "Girl, what do you have to do?" And you say, "Well, I'm trying to make better use of my time." And that person will say, "Oh, girl what are you trying to do?" "Who are you trying to be?"

Now understand, that person is disorganized. So the enemy will try to use someone who is disorganized to disorganize you because he knows this principle.

God is training us now for reigning. He's training us now to be distribution centers. I've discovered that all you've got to do to be a millionaire is change your thinking. If you change your thinking, which includes your judgment, which affects the way you see and do things, you will find that the wealth will come. The only difference is thinking. A person who is making $16,000 a year, or $28,000 a year, thinks totally different from a person who makes $250,000 a year. In the Book of Proverbs, it says, **"For as he thinketh in his heart, so is he" [Proverbs 23:7].**

Here is a word of caution for you. The moment you start thinking like a person who makes $250,000, it is going to separate you from the person who makes $16,000. The people who are in that category will not understand you any more. Folks don't want to separate because Lecretia is there; and Bubba. [No offense to Lecretia and Bubba] They'll say something like, "you know me and Bubba hang together." They don't want to leave. They want to stand around that oak tree and talk about how hard life is. That's not what God has called you to do. Joseph had to leave that group. He thought differently and it separated him.

All you've got to do is change your thinking. Thinking is it. God said, **"For My thoughts are not your thoughts, neither are your ways, My ways" [Isaiah 55:8].** Notice that your ways follow your thoughts. All I had to do was change my thinking. I saw it. And the next thing you know, here comes a big shopping mall because I changed my thinking. Now I'm working on starting an airline. A person came to me after seeing me on a television special to help start an international airline. We're in the process of doing that now. Now, that's all coming to me because I changed my thinking.

The Bible says in Proverbs 30:32, **"if thou hast thought evil, lay thine hand upon thy mouth."** What you think will affect what you say and what you say can affect your life. You will always move in the direction of your most dominant thoughts. This is simple. I believe it's very easy to be a millionaire. All you've got to do is go and meditate the principles of God and apply them in your life. It's not a struggle to get there because even while you're making $28,500 a year, you think on a certain level that makes it no struggle to get there. People who struggle with it are those people who don't know the principles on how to think it before they get there. It'll move you almost without you knowing it. If you think down payments, you'll make down payments; but if you think cash, you'll pay for it cash; my house is paid for, the cars are paid for, everything is paid for. I used to think, if I could just get this down payment. It's all yours, but you can't think outside of your belief.

*What you think will affect what you say and what you say will affect your life. You will always move in the direction of your most dominant thoughts.*

When I talk about being organized, I have to put things in some arrangement that would give me a meaningful relationship that would produce the desired result. A real good scripture for that is found in John, Chapter 6. Remember the feeding of the 5,000? The first thing Jesus said was feed them. And the first thing the disciples said was they didn't know how because they didn't have any money and the resources were not there.

There are three resources that you have: Men, Money, and Minutes. "M, M and M." By Men, I mean men and women. By Money, I mean material things; and by Minutes, I mean time. Those are the three resources that you have. If you manage those resources properly, you'll win every time. The disciples said they didn't have enough, until one of them said there was a lad there [unrecognized resources] who had two fish and five loaves of bread...a two-piece fish dinner. Jesus said that was enough and to bring them to Him. The next thing you know, the food started to multiply. Then Jesus started distributing it to the disciples, and they gave the food to the people.

Notice, Jesus had people to help him. He delegated responsibilities to them so that He could get the job done. So delegation is a key part to organization. You can't do it all yourself. You have to delegate and you have to trust who you delegate to. If you don't trust them, then you will end up micro-managing it. If you do that, then it's just like you doing it yourself again. You'll never grow outside of yourself. What Jesus had to do was feed all of the 5,000 plus women and children. It could have been 20,000 people and Jesus had to feed them before sundown. Here's the key: **God will supernaturally add to your life or your ministry as you are sufficiently organized to contain it**.[8]

Now, organization takes discipline. There are two sides of your brain. One is the right side and the other is the left side. The difference is that the right side is the side of creativity, etc. The left side is analytical, or logical. You bounce between the two sides all of the time. Most people who end up staying where they are, just working a job year after year and never going anywhere, are using the left side of the brain for the most part. So most people in society are left-brain oriented. The right side is creative, intuitive.

There was an idiot savant named Jedidiah Buxton. An idiot savant is a mentally challenged person who possesses some remarkable special aptitude, such as memorization, superior musical ability, or rapid mental mathematical calculation. If you sent Jedidiah to get a loaf of bread at the store, he would turn around and ask you what did you ask him to get. He couldn't contain logical things. Some scientists had a 23-digit number, I believe, and they multiplied it by another 23-digit number, and cubed it by another double digit. By the time they put it in the computer, Jedidiah had the answer because his right brain was functioning over and above what it normally should be. Jedidiah didn't have to figure things, he just intuitively knew it.

Now you see where Adam was in the Garden. That's how Adam could name all the animals and never go to LSU. Before the fall [of mankind] there were no universities; life was not learned, it was discerned. You just knew. Like a movie I saw, where the characters' only getaway vehicle was a helicopter. No training? No problem. They just downloaded the helicopter program and the knowledge to fly it came in an instant. That's the way it's supposed to be. I know people now who have said it just came on them, and they are now playing the piano like Bach or Beethoven, and they said it just happened one morning. Think about it.

My wife and I were coming from Brazil, and I said to her, "Wouldn't it be nice if we stepped off that airplane and the moment we hit that Brazilian soil, we started speaking Portuguese?" It's possible because back at the Tower of Babel, it was only a moment when everyone started speaking a different language. [Genesis 11:7-9] Let's not stop there, let's go to the Book of Acts, where the people were in the upper room and the people started speaking languages they never learned. [Acts 2:3-4] Now if God could do it in Babel and do it on the day of Pentecost, He can do it now. He can give you a language—just download it.

And I know that's the truth; and that's coming. We're getting back up there. When Joel said, "And I [God] will restore to you the years," He went all the way back to Adam. He's not talking about your grandma, He's going all the way back to Adam, **"And I [God] will restore to you the years that the locust hath eaten, the cankerworm..." [Joel 2:25].**

## TIME MANAGEMENT

Why people don't regard time is because basically you don't see time. Time will slip by and you'll never know it. If you are aware of the value of time, you'll find that you'll use time well. Bob Harrison teaches that there are three main dimensions of time.[9] One is "Lopo." Lopo means low payout. If I have some money and I want to invest it in some stocks, I'm looking for an increased return, an increase of about as much as I can get. The same thing holds true for every hour of time you have in a week.

God is checking to see what you do with your time. Bob Harrison also teaches that when you give something for that time, you want the greatest return on that investment as possible. The lowest return is called "Lopo." The highest return is called "Hipo." A medium return is called "Medpo." A negative return, meaning that you were better off to never have done it, is called "Negpo." That's those soap operas on TV. That's when David looked at that woman and saw her on the roof. Because he used his time that way, he got a negative return. It ate up his time, and it ate up his life. If you can't manage your time, you can't manage your money. You will find that they are directly connected.

We became disorganized when Adam fell. Now we're being reorganized. The first step of being born-again is to be organized in the Spirit. The next step is to renew the mind, organize your mind. The final step is to organize your body. Start with these areas to organize your life. Now we're coming back up to where we were before. That's why it says repent. It doesn't mean beat somebody over the head with a bottle. It means return to the top. We're coming back up. It's a powerful thing.

## KEY POINTS

- An effective Leader must be organized, know how to manage their time, and understand how to get work accomplished through others - delegation.
- The structure and organization that exist on an aircraft carrier provide a prime environment for excellence in coordination and teamwork.
- Organization puts you and your environment in the best position for maximum productivity.
- We must even reorganize our thinking to attain the higher levels of achievment.
- It's easy to be a millionaire - just meditate the principles of God and apply them to your life.
- Delegation will help you get more accomplished.
- Before the fall of Adam, man didn't learn, he discerned.
- We became disorganized when Adam fell.
- Getting born-again and renewing your mind will reorganize your thinking as it was meant to be.

# Chapter Seven

# Breaking Through

# CHAPTER SEVEN

## *BREAKING THROUGH TO EFFECTIVE LEADERSHIP*

I often use the example of when man first broke the sound barrier to illustrate what it often takes to break through to new levels in our lives. The test pilot who broke the sound barrier faced all the issues that I've talked about in this book. He had to face fear. Some people thought he was going to disintegrate. Some people were jealous of him and did not want it attempted. He had to get out of his comfort zone and change his traditional thinking about what was possible.

When the test pilot approached the sound barrier, everything began to shake. I remember when I first started to tithe. I started to shake. I said, "Man, I sure hope this works." I had never done that with my paycheck before. Then I learned how to give and each time God would stretch my giving — give this, give that. Now it is easy. Last year we gave more away than I made through my paycheck. I think that's the first time we have ever done that.

So, as the test pilot who broke the sound barrier got closer, everything started shaking. Once he broke through that barrier, everything smoothed out. In every one of our lives, there's a barrier that we're going to have to break. You can tell when you get close to it because it looks like everything around you starts shaking, but if you stay on course, God will take you through, and on the other side it is smooth sailing.

Escaping boxed thinking is probably the greatest step in breaking through to new levels of effective leadership. People who are box thinkers don't choose to think independent of other people. They let other people do all of their thinking for them. They become mindless clones, never fulfilling their creative purpose. Some people have said, "Well, I'm too old" to try this or that. Well, how about the owner and founder of Kentucky Fried Chicken. He was somewhere around 65 years old when he first started the business. Some other people have said, "I'm too young." Stop that! "I'm a woman!" Stop that. You've got to stop that. You've been picking up your input from chickens.

Most people who are box thinkers choose that well-worn path of least resistance. They don't want any resistance. If there's any resistance, they will quit. People who are outside that box, explore new possibilities. They are an elite minority. We've been engineered by God to be creative and successful in this world system. We are supposed to thrive, not survive. A survival mentality is a mentality of the people of the world.

There are three things you've got to have if you want to break through the ceiling of complexity in your life. First, you must change your relationships. Second, change your structure; that is, how you view things and how you are basically oriented and operate. Thirdly, you've got to break your habits–the old pattern of doing things. This is probably the toughest one to do–breaking habit patterns. The way you break them is to not do them all at once. Any bad habits you have in your life, tackle them one at a time. Usually, when you break one, it's tied to a bunch of others.

Below is a testimony of a man that came to my church and who had applied the teachings that he heard me teach. He had a third grade education and had been in prison, but because he was a doer of the Word of God, he broke through the ceiling that society had placed over his life.

"Pastor Winston has been a blessing to my life. I was making $25 every two weeks in 1991. I used to be addicted to dope. I used to be an alcoholic. I got saved in Joliet (Illinois) Prison, but God used Pastor to bless me. I have a third grade education and had to have people write down Pastor's address so that I could come to Living Word Christian Center.

God gave me a job, but God had used Pastor Winston to bless me.

Pastor Winston taught me how to speak to my bills; he told me how to speak to everything. I live in a quarter of a million dollar home. I have a new Mercedes Benz sitting outside. Pastor taught me how to speak and 'call those things which be not as though they were.' He taught me that.

At 6:30 in the morning, I used to ride the train going to work, [I don't work there any more], and I used to listen to him [Pastor]. I listened to him when he said he worked at IBM. I spoke to my bills, I didn't ask anybody for nothing. I am fixing to buy a new Rolls Royce in July. I make $30,000 a month in my business. I have a third grade education—this is true, but I'm saying this—and I'm coming back, listen to your pastor, but the Bible says, “I [God] can take the foolish things and confound the wise.” [1 Corinthians 1:27] A man with a third grade education, look at what God has done for me. I got seven bedrooms, 4 bathrooms with Jacuzzis, a stereo system building, a kitchen downstairs and upstairs.

I’m going to say this, Pastor Winston, I didn’t have any money in the bank. Listen to this. I did what you told me. I waited until my wife and kids left. I said, ‘Honey, you all go to church.’ I began to speak that law into existence. I said, ‘You hear me calling you—$250,000 loan—come here! You hear me calling you!’ I began to say, “Faith comes by hearing and hearing by the word of God.” I spoke that thing under authority, under the anointing of God and I heard you [Pastor] say, ‘Don’t let up.’ The enemy came in all kinds of ways, but I held on to what you [Pastor] said. I got money in the bank. I got three cars...”

And the testimony goes on. Glory to God!

## Key Points

- In every one of our lives, there's a barrier that we're going to have to break.
- You can tell when you get close to your barrier because it looks like everything around you starts shaking.
- Boxed thinking prevents us from exploring new possibilities and creative solutions.
- Breaking through the barrier requires changes in your relationships, your manner of operation, and your habits.
- If a man with a third grade education can obtain a business bringing in $30,000 a month, what's my excuse?

# CONCLUSION

I trust that this book has stirred a desire in you to move out of the box and break through to effective leadership. I pray that you will pursue at all costs the purpose and calling that God has for your life and that you will not let the devil steal your dreams and what God has given you.

You may ask, what does it mean to "Develop the Spirit of Leadership?" Let me give you an example that may illustrate this concept. Have you ever witnessed a minister or speaker who has spent time being mentored under a powerful leader? (Kind of like Elijah and Elisha.) He talks like his mentor, uses teachings and illustrations from that mentor, and even sometimes walks and gestures like that mentor. Why? Because he has spent so much time learning from the mentor that he has picked up the mentor's "spirit." I'm not talking about something spooky, but you can always tell what kind of people someone is hanging around because they pick up qualities and characteristics of that influence.

**"Now when they saw the boldness of Peter and John, and perceived that they were unlearned and ignorant men, they marvelled; and they took knowledge of them, that they had been with Jesus." [Acts 4:13]**

That's what I mean when I say "Developing the Spirit of Leadership." Spend time in God's Word learning from the leaders He has used and developed. Let the Holy Spirit make them come alive to you as they make choices to follow God and step out in faith and not compromise under pressure.

This book is meant to take you to another level, to stir up the potential of leadership in you. Receive this teaching and apply it to your life. If there is anything that needs to be dealt with in your life, resolve today that you're going to deal with it. You can be an effective leader. God is calling for effective leaders and anointed leaders.

And remember, you are not waiting on God. God is waiting on you.

# FOOTNOTES

[1] Definition of a *Leader* taken from Random House Dictionary of the English Language, College Edition c. 1969 by Random House

[2] Covey, Stephen R., *The 7 Habits of Highly Effective People*; Simon & Schuster, 1990

[3] Hilliard, Dr. I.V., Tape Series - *Minister's Conference 2000*; New Light Christian Center Church, Houston, Texas

[4] Copeland, Germaine, *Prayers that Avail Much*; Harrison House, 1997

[5] Dufresne, Ed, *Praying God's Word*; Whitaker House, 1992

[6] Maxwell, John, *The 21 Irrefutable Laws of Leadership*; Thomas Nelson, 1998

[7] Munroe, Dr. Myles, *Understanding Your Potential*; Destiny Image Publishers, 1992

[8] Hammond, Mac, Tape Series - *Mac Hammond on Leadership*; Mac Hammond Ministries, Minneapolis, Minnesota

[9] Harrison, Bob, Tape Series - *Time Management*; Harrison International, Tulsa, Oklahoma

## About the Author

William S. Winston
Bill Winston Ministries, Founder and President
Living Word Christian Center, Founder and Pastor
Chairman of the Board of Directors, New Covenant Community Bank

William S. Winston is a visionary leader with an insightful awareness of what people need to succeed and how he can empower them for success.

After serving in the United States Air Force, where he received awards for superior flying skills, Bill joined the IBM Corporation as a marketing representative. His exceptional managerial and relational skills rapidly earned him positions with increasing responsibility within the organization. When he resigned in 1985, he was a regional marketing manager in IBM's Midwest Region and was responsible for more than $35 million in sales revenue per year.

Following what he believed was a higher purpose for his life, Bill founded the Mission Temple of Faith Church in Minneapolis, Minnesota in December 1984. In the pursuing years, he attended Logos Bible School and Oral Roberts University Graduate School of Theology.

In 1989, Bill moved to Chicago and became pastor of Living Word Church. Within one year, church growth necessitated a move to a larger facility and the congregation relocated to

Forest Park, Illinois and changed its name to Living Word Christian Center. Continued congregational growth led to the purchase of the 33-acre Forest Park Mall in 1998. The congregation completely renovated a movie cinema complex in the Mall into a multimillion state-of-the-art worship center.

In addition, Living Word Christian Center established a broad range of ministry enterprises, including a bookstore, Bible training center, private elementary school, The Joseph Center® School of Business and Entrepreneurship, and a recording company. Bill is the host of the Believer's Walk of Faith, a daily Bill Winston Ministries radio and television program which is broadcast internationally. Living Word Christian Center employs over 130 full-time and part-time staff, has 13,000+ members, and is supported by approximately 50 volunteer helps ministries.

A licensed commercial pilot and an ordained minister, Bill is also a graduate of Tuskegee University and attended the Northwestern University Kellogg Graduate School of Management. He is married to Veronica Brown and is the father of three children, Melody, Nicole, and David.

## PRAYER FOR SALVATION AND BAPTISM IN THE HOLY SPIRIT

Heavenly Father, I come to You in the Name of Your Son Jesus Christ. You said in Your Word that whosoever shall call upon the Name of the Lord shall be saved (Romans 10:13). Father, I am calling on Jesus right now. I believe He died on the cross for my sins, that He was raised from the dead on the third day, and He's alive right now. Lord Jesus, I am asking You now, come into my heart. Live Your life in me and through me. I repent of my sins and surrender myself totally and completely to You. Heavenly Father, by faith I now confess Jesus Christ as my new Lord and Savior from this day forward, I dedicate my life to serving Him.

Now Heavenly Father, I am Your child, for I believe in my heart that Jesus has been raised from the dead and I have confessed Him as my Lord.

Jesus said, "How much more shall your heavenly Father give the Holy Spirit to those who ask Him." I ask You now in the Name of Jesus to fill me with the Holy Spirit. I step into the fullness and power that I desire in the Name of Jesus. I confess that I am a Spirit-filled Christian. As I yield my vocal organs, I expect to speak in tongues for the Spirit gives me utterance in the Name of Jesus. Praise the Lord! Amen.

## Books by Bill Winston

The Power of the Tithe
Power of Grace
The Spirit of Leadership
Born-Again and Spirit-Filled

## BILL WINSTON MINISTRIES

***We'd like to hear from you!***

For more information about Bill Winston Ministries and a free product catalog, please write to us or visit us on the worldwide web at:

Bill Winston Ministries
P.O. Box 947
Oak Park, Illinois 60303-0947
708-697-5100
800-711-9327

www.bwm.org